MY FIRST TRIP TO A
BASEBALL GAME

By Katie Kawa

Gareth Stevens
Publishing

Please visit our website, www.garethstevens.com. For a free color catalog of all our high-quality books, call toll free 1-800-542-2595 or fax 1-877-542-2596.

Library of Congress Cataloging-in-Publication Data

Kawa, Katie.
My first trip to a baseball game / Katie Kawa.
    p. cm. — (My first adventures)
Includes index.
ISBN 978-1-4339-7304-8 (pbk.)
ISBN 978-1-4339-7305-5 (6-pack)
ISBN 978-1-4339-7307-9 (library binding)
1. Baseball—Juvenile literature. I. Title.
GV867.5.K385 2012
796.357—dc23

                                        2011043597

First Edition

Published in 2013 by
Gareth Stevens Publishing
111 East 14th Street, Suite 349
New York, NY 10003

Copyright © 2013 Gareth Stevens Publishing

Editor: Katie Kawa
Designer: Andrea Davison-Bartolotta

All Illustrations by Planman Technologies

Printed in the United States of America

CPSIA compliance information: Batch #CS12GS: For further information contact Gareth Stevens, New York, New York at 1-800-542-2595.

Contents

Today I am going
to a baseball game.

My family and I go
to the baseball park.
This is where
our team plays.

My dad holds
our tickets.
They tell us
where to sit.

We get food to eat.
My mom and dad
eat hot dogs.

I get ice cream.

The game is lots of fun!

First, one player throws the ball. He is called the pitcher.

Then, a player hits the ball. He is called the batter.

One player hits the ball
over the wall.
It is a home run!

21

Our team won
the game!

Words to Know

batter

pitcher

tickets

Index